MW00647237

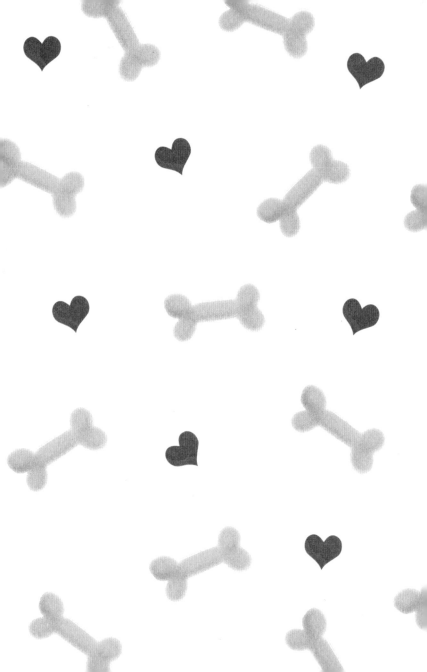

The Truth About
DOG PEOPLE

ISBN: 978-1-68088-427-2 (previously ISBN: 978-1-68088-342-8)

◪ and Blue Mountain Press are registered in U.S. Patent and Trademark Office. Certain trademarks are used under license.

Printed in China.
First printing of this edition: 2022

♲ This book is printed on recycled paper.

This book is printed on paper that has been specially produced to be acid free (neutral pH) and contains no groundwood or unbleached pulp. It conforms with the requirements of the American National Standards Institute, Inc., so as to ensure that this book will last and be enjoyed by future generations.

Blue Mountain Arts, Inc.
P.O. Box 4549, Boulder, Colorado 80306

The Truth About
DOG PEOPLE

Jo Renfro

Blue Mountain Press™
Boulder, Colorado

Dog People wake up early.
Oh, so early.

They have slobbery faces
from slobbery kisses.

Dog People
have hairy clothes...

...and hairy houses
with muddy floors.

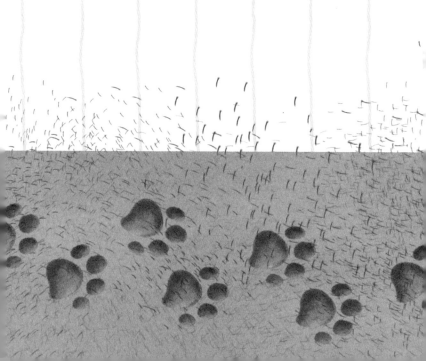

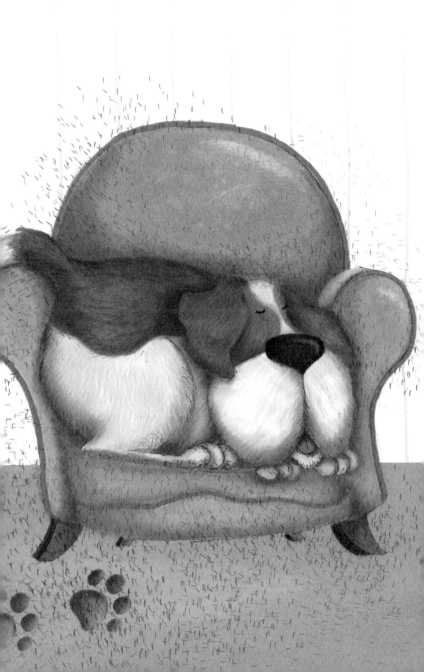

They talk to their dogs
like they're old friends.

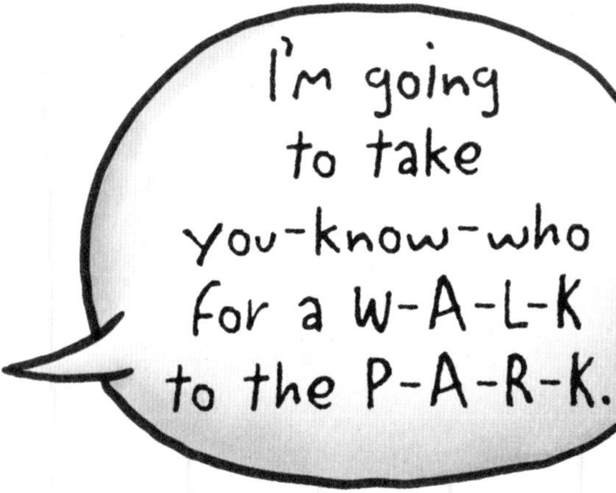
I'm going to take you-know-who for a W-A-L-K to the P-A-R-K.

Dog People
are good spellers.

They walk in the rain...

...and in the snow,
even when they'd rather
be home on the couch.

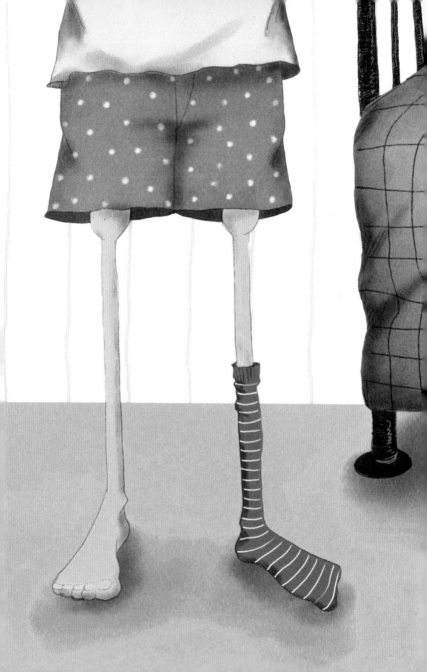

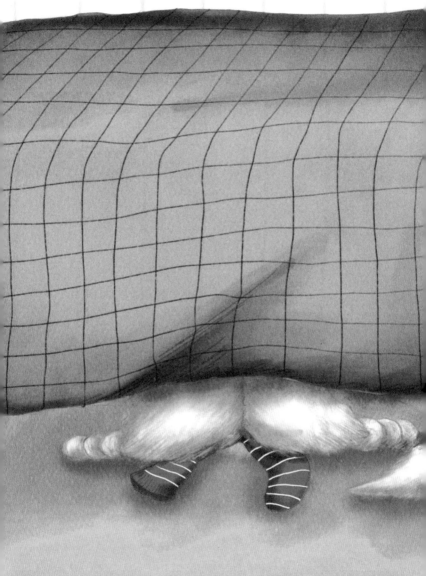

Dog People are patient...

...and they
make friends easily.

Dog People pick up sticks and toys and whatever is left of their slippers.

They pick up
all sorts of things.

Dog People
share their beds...
and their dinners.

They are never lonely.
Seriously... never.

Dog People don't mind the rain or the mud or even the hairy clothes, because they get to hang out with dogs.

And even when they're sick or tired or crabby or lazy, their dogs are there for them.

Their dogs love them.
No. Matter. What.

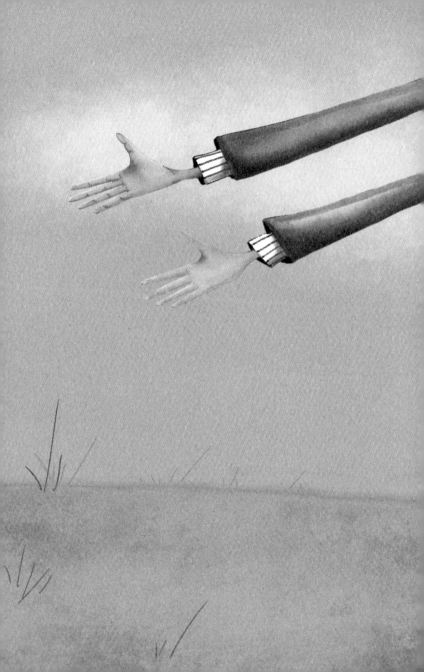

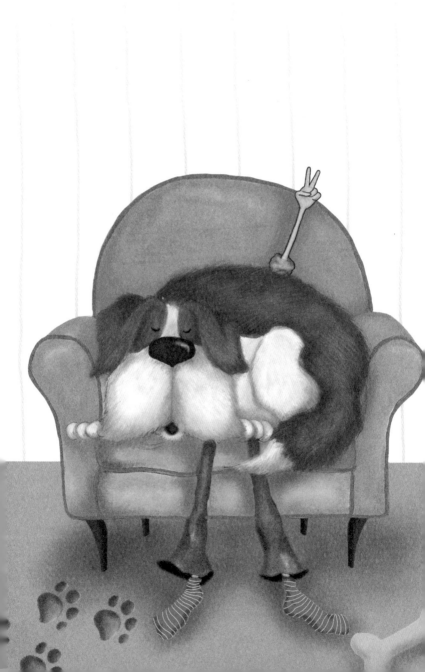

So take it from dogs
and their people... and

LOVE

unconditionally.

About the Author

Jo Renfro is a freelance writer and illustrator with a passion for mixing color, pattern, and whimsy in her somewhat quirky, often amusing, and always upbeat work.

She enjoys using her sense of humor developed from raising three kids, several dogs, numerous cats, and a potbellied pig named Matilda to create pieces that are lightheartedly inspirational.

Her love of the outdoors, animals, and her amazing kids is often reflected in her work.

A lifelong Kansan, she recently moved to Colorado to be close to the mountains, which still take her breath away every single day.